Study Guide to Accompany

What Is Economics?

Third Edition

Study Guide to Accompany

What Is Economics?

Third Edition

James V. Pinto
Professor of Economics
Northern Arizona University

Bristlecone Books

Mayfield Publishing Company
Mountain View, California
London • Toronto

ISBN 1-55934-235-8

Manufactured in the United States of America

10 9 8 7 6 5 4 3 2

Bristlecone Books
Mayfield Publishing Company
1240 Villa Street
Mountain View, California 94041

CONTENTS

To Kay, Nick, Kelsey, and Vincent

Chapter 1

WHAT IS ECONOMICS?

IMPORTANT TERMS AND CONCEPTS

capital goods
command system
decent material standard
   of living
economic freedom
economic problem
economics
entrepreneur
fair distribution of income
financial capital
full employment
growth

labor
land
law of increasing costs
management
market economy
opportunity costs
price stability
production-possibilities
   curve
quality environment
resources
traditional system

COMPLETION QUESTIONS

Fill in the blanks with the proper word or words from the list
above. Not all terms are used.

1. A(n) _command system_ is characterized by centralized au-
    thority and decision making.

2. In a(n) _market economy_ people are motivated by the eco-
    nomic rewards within a process of exchange.

3. _opportunity costs_ measure(s) the true costs or sacrifices that
    are made when engaging in any type of activity.

4. The decision makers in a(n) _traditional system_ rely on cus-
    tom or tradition to answer the economic questions.

5. When people speak of capital as money they are actually
    referring to _financial capital_

6. The economic goal of a(n) _quality environment_ deals with the
    problems created by pollution.

7. The economic goal of a(n) _fair distribution of income_ does not mean
    an absolutely equal distribution.

8. To many people the goal of *economic* _freedom_ would work best in a decentralized, free-enterprise system.

9. _capital goods_ is(are) man-made, can be reproduced or replaced, and tend(s) to increase the productivity of labor.

10. The _curve_ *Productive possibility* shows all the various choices open to a society when considering alternative uses for economic resources.

11. The phenomenon of the _cost_ *law of increasing* reflects the fact that resources are not perfectly interchangeable in all types of production.

12. The primary economic goal for all societies is a(n) *decent material standard of living* for all citizens.

13. The fact that it is wasteful to have unused resources in a society reflects the economic goal of _full employment_.

14. The economic goal of _stability_ *price* would not result in inflation or deflation.

15. The _problem_ *economic* is how best to use scarce economic resources.

CROSSWORD PUZZLE

Fill in the crossword puzzle from the list of Important Terms and Concepts. Not all of the terms are used.

ACROSS
1. Every natural resource above, on, or below the soil.
2. The science of making choices.
3. The lack of this may cause hunger and starvation.
5. Coordinates and organizes all other resources.

DOWN
1. The primary national economic resource.
2. Managers.
4. Limited in nature and organized in many ways.

TRUE AND FALSE

_F_ 1. The economic resource of land is made up only of soil.

_T_ 2. Money is neither a capital good nor an economic resource.

_T_ 3. An uneven distribution of incomes is often a result of differences in education, intelligence, and skills.

_F_ 4. A traditional system tends to be very dynamic, with high levels of economic well-being.

_F_ 5. The European democratic socialist systems are characterized by dictatorships.

_T_ 6. The market system is decentralized, using prices for decision-making guidelines.

_T_ 7. Economists look at the sacrifices that must be made when the economic resources are used in alternative ways.

_F_ 8. The true costs of any one action are the explicit accounting costs only.

_F_ 9. A fundamental law in economics is the law of decreasing costs.

MULTIPLE CHOICE

1. All nations would like to see all, or nearly all, of their available resources being used. This reflects the economic goal of
   a. full employment
   b. price stability
   c. economic growth
   d. quality environment
   e. fair distribution of income

2. The victims of inflation include people on fixed incomes, savers, and lenders. Which economic goal is not being met?
   a. full employment
   b. price stability
   c. economic growth
   d. quality environment
   e. fair distribution of income

3. There are critics who argue that the United States is presently overdeveloped and that we would benefit by not adding any more to our economic affluence. These critics are against which economic goal?

   a. quality environment
   b. fair distribution of income
   c. economic growth
   d. price stability
   e. full employment

4. "Total equality would be unrealistic and probably undesirable because it would destroy healthy economic incentives." Instead of this position, which of the following economic goals should a society seek?

   a. full employment
   b. price stability
   c. economic growth
   d. quality environment
   e. fair distribution of income

5. The ability of workers to choose occupations commensurate with their skills and experience reflects which of these economic goals?

   a. full employment
   b. centralized decision making
   c. economic freedom
   d. economic growth
   e. regional planning

6. The values of economics are primarily _____ values.
   a. social
   b. material
   c. religious
   d. political
   e. ethical

7. According to the law of increasing costs, each additional unit of Good A added to production will result in what happening to the production of Good B?

   a. It stays constant.
   b. It increases.
   c. It decreases, with constant losses in production.
   d. It decreases, with decreasing losses in production.
   e. It decreases, with increasing losses in production.

8. "Competitive, interdependent, and self-regulating" describes what type of economic system?

   a. market
   b. command
   c. traditional
   d. democratic socialism
   e. all types of economic systems

9. What are the advantages of a traditional economic system?

   a. supply and demand markets
   b. collective decision making
   c. centralized decision making
   d. little conflict
   e. none of the above

PROBLEMS AND DISCUSSION

1. Use the following diagram to show a production-possibilities curve. Explain why this curve has the shape that it does.

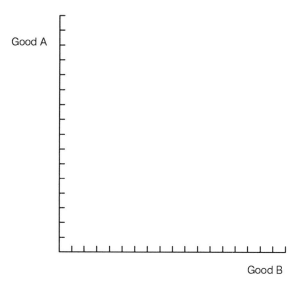

2. Of the several economic goals, list and discuss different pairs that you feel are in conflict. Why are they in conflict?

3. Table 1-1 shows the production possibilities for two commodities, pizzas and waterbeds. Using information from the table, solve problems (a) and (b).

Table 1-1

Combination	Pizzas	Waterbeds
A	0	5
B	8	4
C	15	3
D	21	2
E	26	1
F	30	0

(a) On the following figure, construct a production-possibilities curve based on the information contained in Table 1-1.

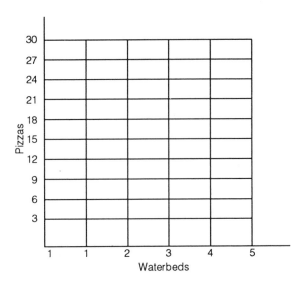

(b) Fill in Table 1-2, showing the opportunity cost (in terms of pizzas forgone) of producing the first through the fifth waterbed.

Table 1-2

Waterbeds	Opportunity Cost (pizzas forgone)
1	_____
2	_____
3	_____
4	_____
5	_____

4. Sometimes the distinction between land and capital is hard to determine. How would you classify the following items? Why?

(a) a farm animal used in production

(b) a fish in the ocean

(c) water in a natural lake

(d) distilled water used in an auto battery

Chapter 1
ANSWERS

COMPLETION QUESTIONS

1. command system
2. market economy
3. opportunity costs
4. traditional system
5. financial capital
6. quality environment
7. fair distribution of income
8. economic freedom
9. capital goods
10. production-possibilities curve
11. law of increasing costs
12. decent material standard of living
13. full employment
14. price stability
15. economic problem

CROSSWORD PUZZLE

TRUE AND FALSE

1. false
2. true
3. true
4. false
5. false

6. true
7. true
8. false
9. false

MULTIPLE CHOICE

1. a
2. b
3. c
4. e
5. c

6. b
7. e
8. a
9. d

PROBLEMS AND DISCUSSION

1.

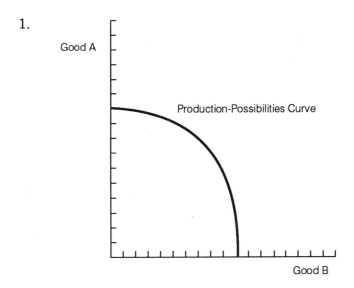

The production-possibilities curve is shaped the way it is (convex, looking down from above) because of the law of increasing costs. This law holds because all resources are not perfectly interchangeable from one type of production to another.

2. List of economic goals in conflict:

a. Price stability and full employment: The nearer the economy is to full employment of resources, the more likely it is that the prices paid for those resources will increase. This may increase the cost of production and lead to price increases for final goods.

b. Price stability and growth: The faster the economy grows, the more likely it is there will be bottlenecks in the resource markets that can lead to higher prices being paid for those resources. This may increase the cost of production and lead to price increases for final goods.

c. Growth and quality environment: The faster the economy grows, the more likely it is that there will be pollution from the industrial sector of the economy. The controls and regulations necessary to combat pollution may lead to less production (slower economic growth).

3. (a)

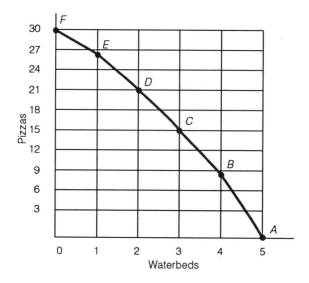

(b)

Waterbeds	Opportunity Cost (pizzas forgone)
1	4(30–26)
2	5(26–21)
3	6(21–15)
4	7(15–8)
5	8(8–0)

Combination F shows a production of 0 waterbeds and 30 pizzas. To produce the first waterbed would require a movement along the production possibilities curve to combination E. At E, only 26 pizzas can be produced. So the opportunity cost of producing the first waterbed is the number of pizzas that *are not produced*—in this case, 4 pizzas (30–26).

4. Classification:

(a) A farm animal should be considered capital. It is a living resource but not human; thus it cannot be classified as labor. For the animal to be productive, it must be trained; therefore, it is not a "natural" resource under the classification of land.

(b) A fish in the ocean would be classified as a natural resource and fall under the classification of land. It is a living (or biological) resource but not human (not labor). Man has not modified, educated, or trained the fish to fit into a productive system; therefore, it is not capital.

(c) The water in a natural lake is classified as land.

(d) Distilled water used in an auto battery is classified as capital. Distilled water does not occur in nature, thus it cannot be classified as land but must be modified by man before its use in the battery. Once man modifies a natural resource, it is more properly known as a raw material. There is much debate on whether a raw material should be classified as land or capital.

Chapter 2

THE U.S. ECONOMY

IMPORTANT TERMS AND CONCEPTS

absolute advantage
cartel
communism
comparative advantage
competition
concentration
entry barrier
government regulation
invisible hand
maximization
monopoly

natural abilities
natural monopoly
nonprice competition
oligopoly
private ownership
regional monopoly
self-interest
Sherman Antitrust Act
specialization
voucher system

COMPLETION QUESTIONS

Fill in the blanks with the proper word or words from the list above. Not all terms are used.

1. A(n) _natural monopoly_ exists when it is inefficient and very costly for another firm to exist within the same industry.

2. _government regulations_ is necessary to counteract the power of natural monopolists.

3. The only drug store in a small, isolated town would be an example of a(n) _regional monopoly_

4. In his book, *Inquiry into the Nature and Courses of the Wealth of Nations*, Adam Smith said that each individual (or business) pursuing his own self-interest is "led by a(n) _invisible hand_ to promote the end which is not part of his intention."

5. Under the _Sherman Antitrust act_ it is illegal to conspire to form a monopoly.

6. Milton Friedman has suggested a(n) _voucher system_ to bring competition into the educational system.

specialyation

7. _____ can be worthwhile even when an individual has superior skills in several areas.

8. A country has a(n) _absolute advantage_ compared with another if its workers are more efficient in the production of all goods considered.

9. Even if worker Jones is more efficient in the production of all products, worker Smith will have a(n) _comparative advantage_ in the production of certain products.

10. If much of our high productivity and efficiency in the U.S. economy comes from specialization and division of labor, the motivation to do all this work comes from _self interest_.

CROSSWORD PUZZLE

Fill in the crossword puzzle from the list of Important Terms and Concepts. Not all terms are used.

ACROSS

1. Market type where all sellers face the same price.
3. Results in greater output than when not used.
6. Only one seller in the market.
7. Characterized by price leadership.

DOWN

1. Pure competition has the least what?
2. The goal of firms with respect to profits.
4. Competing companies divide a market or set prices.
5. The production distribution philosophy by K. Marx.

TRUE AND FALSE

__T__ 1. One of the major features of oligopoly is entry barriers.

__T__ 2. The monopolist will charge a higher price than a firm in pure competition producing the same good.

__F__ 3. Under the capitalist system, the big firms often get smaller; i.e., there is a decentralization of economic power over time.

__F__ 4. The United States government holds a legal monopoly over all types of mail and packages.

__F__ 5. Pure competition is characterized by a small number of relatively large firms.

__T__ 6. The best example of a competitive industry in the United States is farming.

__T__ 7. Socialism means that businesses are owned by the public.

__F__ 8. Political despotism cannot thrive in a capitalist state.

__F__ 9. The self-interest of businesses is to maximize the material satisfaction achieved through consumption.

__F__ 10. The voucher system was developed by Adam Smith.

MULTIPLE CHOICE

1. Some economists feel that we overspecialize despite the gains we receive as a result of comparative advantage. One drawback of specialization is

14

a. absolute advantage
b. higher productivity
c. the psychological toll
d. division of labor
e. none of the above

2. In reality our system of supply and demand is often not allowed to regulate itself. Which of the following usually interferes with the system?

   a. consumers
   b. producers
   c. resource owners
   d. governments
   e. none of the above

3. In a market economy, regulation and allocation take place when _____ operates for every good and service that has economic value.

   a. self-interest behavior
   b. comparative advantage exchange
   c. absolute advantage exchange
   d. government regulation policy
   e. supply and demand

4. One of the major features of oligopoly is entry barriers. These may include

   a. the cost of real capital goods
   b. massive marketing problems
   c. advertising costs
   d. all of the above
   e. none of the above

5. An example of an oligopolistic industry is

   a. steel
   b. public utilities
   c. farming
   d. retail
   e. wholesale

6. A monopoly is characterized by

   a. a large number of small firms
   b. no close substitutes for the product sold
   c. much competitive advertising
   d. no entry barriers

   e. lower prices than those charged in a competitive industry

7. A purely competitive industry is characterized by
   a. a single seller
   b. much advertising
   c. no single seller with any control over price
   d. difficulty in entering the industry
   e. a small number of large firms

8. Surprisingly, the most "communistic" institution is
   a. the family
   b. farming
   c. education
   d. sports
   e. government

9. The self-interest of workers is to
   a. maximize profits
   b. maximize revenues from the sale of final goods
   c. maximize income
   d. minimize their material satisfaction
   e. none of the above

10. Under this system no economic dictatorship tells people what to do with their economic lives.
   a. a market system
   b. fascism
   c. communism
   d. socialism
   e. all of the above

PROBLEMS AND DISCUSSION

1. Given the information below, how would you answer the question, "Which industry would most likely be a monopolist?" Explain why.

Industry A	Industry B
Price of good $x = P_x = \$1$	$P_x = \$2$
Quantity of good $x = Q_x = 3$ units	$Q_x = 2$ units

2. Make a case for and against advertising for the market structures of (a) pure competition, (b) oligopoly, and (c) pure monopoly.

3. Karl Marx believed that the communist state of the future could offer a utopian situation to its citizens; i.e., there would be no scarcity of goods and services. In the absence of scarcity of goods and services, is there a need for the study of economics?

COMPLETION QUESTIONS

1. natural monopoly
2. government regulation
3. regional monopoly
4. invisible hand
5. Sherman Antitrust Act

6. voucher system
7. specialization
8. absolute advantage
9. comparative advantage
10. self-interest

CROSSWORD PUZZLE

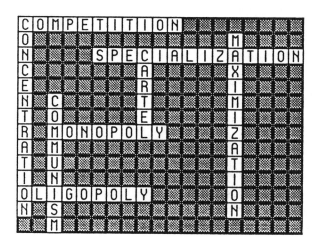

TRUE AND FALSE

1. true
2. true
3. false
4. false
5. false

6. true
7. true
8. false
9. false
10. false

MULTIPLE CHOICE

1. c	6. b
2. d	7. c
3. e	8. a
4. d	9. c
5. a	10. a

PROBLEMS AND DISCUSSION

1. Industry B is the most likely to be a monopolist, because it is charging a higher price for good x than Industry A. In addition, industry B is offering less in the marketplace than Industry A.

2. a. The firm in pure competition has no incentive to advertise, since the consumers of its product consider the products produced by firms in the purely competitive industry to be identical. Advertisement would simply add to the firm's production costs.

b. The firm in differentiated oligopoly uses advertising as a way of competing with other firms in the industry. It avoids price competition in order to lower the risks in doing business. The firm in an undifferentiated oligopoly also has no incentive for engaging in competitive advertising for the same reasons as the businesses in pure competition.

c. The firm with a pure monopoly usually has no economic incentive to advertise because it has no competing firms to worry about.

3. At first glance, Marx's utopian society with unlimited goods and services would eliminate the need for the study of economics. Even in such a system, however, time is a scarce commodity because people do not live forever. Since our time on earth is limited, we must make choices concerning how best to allocate it, even if there were no scarcity of goods and services. Since individuals would still be required to make choices, the study of economics would be justified.

Chapter 3

SUPPLY AND DEMAND

IMPORTANT TERMS AND CONCEPTS

black market
businessperson's definition
  of elasticity
complements
cost of production
demand
demand curve
economist's definition
  of elasticity
effective demand
elastic
equilibrium
income effect
inelastic
inferior good
law of downward-
  sloping demand

normal good
price ceiling
price elasticity
rationing
real income
shortage
substitutes
substitution effect
supply
supply curve
support price
surplus
tastes
technological
  advancement

COMPLETION QUESTIONS

Fill in the blanks with the proper word or words from the list above. Not all terms are used.

1. Your _effect demand_ for a product will be made evident only when you actually go out and buy it.

2. By observing the quantity of goods bought at a variety of prices, we can work out what is called the _demand curve_ in the form of a graph.

3. A lower price will increase your _real income_ or purchasing power.

4. A(n) _normal_ _good_ is one that consumers tend to buy more of as their income increases.

5. A(n) _supply_ _curve_ shows how much suppliers would like to provide at different prices.

6. A(n) _support_ _price_ means that the government will guarantee the farmers a price above the equilibrium price.

7. _price_ _elasticy_ measures the responsiveness of the quantity demanded to price changes.

8. The total revenue change due to a change in price is given by the _business person definition of elasticity_

9. The percentage change in the quantity demanded divided by the percentage change in price is given by the _economics definition of elasticity_

10. That point above which it is illegal to charge is called a(n) _price ceiling_

11. An illegal market that usually results from a price ceiling is a(n) _black market_

12. The greater someone's real income the more likely he or she will purchase more of all goods, including the good under consideration. We call this the _income effect_

13. The gain in total satisfaction if we substitute a cheaper good for a higher-priced one is due to the _substitution effect_

14. The _law of sloping demand_ states that there is an inverse relationship between price and the quantity demanded.

15. A(n) _inferior_ _good_ is one consumers tend to buy less of as their income increases.

CROSSWORD PUZZLE

Fill in the crossword puzzle from the list of Important Terms and Concepts. Not all terms are used.

ACROSS
1. Used together in consumption.
3. When quantity demanded is not very responsive.
5. Preferences for consuming a good.
7. Quantity supplied greater than quantity demanded.
8. To produce and make available in a market.
9. Alternative to prices being free to function.
10. Means much more than just desiring a product.

DOWN

2. When the quantity demanded is very responsive.
4. Mutual satisfaction of suppliers and demanders.
6. Used in place of each other in consumption.
7. Quantity demanded greater than quantity supplied.

TRUE AND FALSE

___F___ 1. The lower the price, the less the quantity demanded.

___F___ 2. A change in the price of a good will shift its demand curve.

___T___ 3. The demand for cars tends to go down if the price of gasoline goes up significantly.

___F___ 4. Changes in tastes and fashion cause a supply curve to shift.

___T___ 5. Most supply curves are upward sloping.

___T___ 6. Perhaps the major cause for an increase in supply is technological advancement.

___T___ 7. In an unimpeded market, the price has complete freedom to move to equilibrium.

___F___ 8. A price ceiling in an agricultural market will generally cause a surplus.

___F___ 9. Black markets result from price supports.

___T___ 10. A change in the number of buyers will shift a demand curve.

MULTIPLE CHOICE

1. Effective demand includes the idea that
   a. you are willing and able to purchase the good
   b. the effect of the purchase will be good
   c. the demand will make a difference
   d. goods are substitutable in consumption
   e. most goods are normal goods

2. Price elasticity of demand is
   a. the absolute change in demand divided by the absolute change in price
   b. the absolute change in the quantity demanded divided by the absolute change in price
   c. the percentage change in demand divided by the absolute change in price
   d. the percentage change in profits divided by the percentage change in sales
   e. the percentage change in the quantity demanded divided by the percentage change in price

3. Some general principles for determining inelastic demand include which of the following?
   a. It's a necessary good.
   b. It's a small part of one's budget.
   c. There are few substitutes in consumption.
   d. All of the above
   e. None of the above

4. If the demand for a good is elastic, then an increase in the price of that good will
   a. raise total revenue
   b. lower total revenue
   c. leave total revenue unchanged
   d. cause per unit cost to fall
   e. cause per unit cost to rise

5. If the total area of the total revenue rectangle under a demand curve gets smaller as price falls, then demand is
   a. inelastic
   b. elastic
   c. normal
   d. inferior
   e. none of the above

6. An elasticity of 2.5 means
   a. that a 1 percent increase in price will cause a 2.5 percent increase in the quantity demanded
   b. that a 10 percent decrease in price will cause a 25 percent decrease in the quantity demanded
   c. that a 1 percent decrease in price will cause a 2.5 percent increase in the quantity demanded

24

d. all of the above

e. none of the above

7. The income effect reflects

a. unadjusted money income

b. real income

c. the willingness to react to changes in relative prices

d. a supply curve

e. the law of diminishing returns

8. The substitution effect reflects

a. reaction to changes in relative prices

b. money income

c. real income

d. normal goods

e. inferior goods

9. If the price of a substitute good increases, then the demand for the good under consideration will

a. stay constant

b. decrease

c. increase

d. have a flatter slope

e. have a steeper slope

10. An outward shift in the supply curve means that at a given price

a. a small quantity will be supplied

b. demand will decrease

c. the quantity demanded will increase

d. a larger quantity will be supplied

e. a small quantity will be consumed

PROBLEMS AND DISCUSSION

1. Use Table 3-1 to plot information on the figure that is provided. Then answer questions a through d.

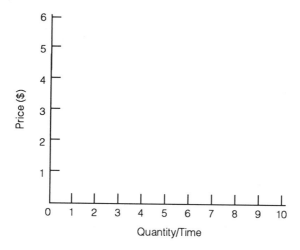

Table 3-1

Quantity Supplied Q_s	Price P $	Quantity Demanded Q_D
10	5	2
8	4	4
6	3	6
4	2	8
2	1	10

a. What is the equilibrium price?

b. What is the equilibrium quantity?

c. What would be the surplus if the price were fixed at
   P = $4?

d. What would be the shortage if the price were fixed at
   P = $2?

2. List the factors that can shift (a) the demand curve and (b)
the supply curve. Why are we able to place both the supply
curve and the demand curve on the same diagram?

3. Given the following data, what must the price of gasoline
be to result in a decrease in the quantity demanded of 20
percent? When using the elasticity formula, figure the percentage changes by dividing by the initial price or initial
quantity as necessary.

   a. Price elasticity of demand for gasoline is 0.45.
   b. 30,500 million gallons of gasoline are consumed per
      year.
   c. The price of gasoline is $1.20 per gallon.

4. What would be the policy implications for a federal farm
program if it is found that the demand for wheat is relatively
inelastic?

Chapter 3
ANSWERS

COMPLETION QUESTIONS

1. effective demand
2. demand curve
3. real income
4. normal good
5. supply curve
6. support price
7. price elasticity
8. businessperson's definition of elasticity
9. economist's definition of elasticity
10. price ceiling
11. black market
12. income effect
13. substitution effect
14. law of downward-sloping demand
15. inferior good

CROSSWORD PUZZLE

TRUE AND FALSE

1. false	6. true
2. false	7. true
3. true	8. false
4. false	9. false
5. true	10. true

MULTIPLE CHOICE

1. a	6. c
2. e	7. b
3. d	8. a
4. b	9. c
5. a	10. d

PROBLEMS AND DISCUSSION

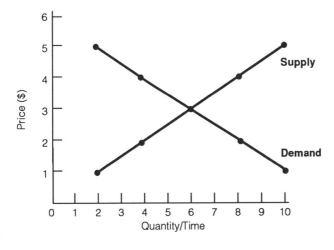

1. a. $3
   b. 6 units
   c. surplus = 4 units
   d. shortage = 4 units

can shift a demand curve are

substitute or complement

g
buyers

can shift the supply curve are
1. number of suppliers
2. changes in technology
3. cost of production

We can place both a supply curve and a demand curve in the same two-dimensional diagram because they are both related to price and quantity. On the demand side, it is the price and the quantity demanded. On the supply side, it is the price and the quantity supplied.

3. price elasticity of demand =

$$\frac{\text{percent change in quantity demanded}}{\text{percent change in price}}$$

$$0.45 = \frac{0.20}{\text{percent change in price}}$$

percent change in price = .20/0.45 = 0.44

price of gasoline = $1.20

$1.20 x 0.44 = 0.53

total new price = $1.73

4. If the demand for wheat is relatively inelastic, then the total revenue rule indicates that for the farmer to have more income (increase total revenue), price must be raised. The government would want to enact policies designed to raise the price of wheat. These programs might include price supports or production controls.

Chapter 4

BUSINESSES AND HOUSEHOLDS

IMPORTANT TERMS AND CONCEPTS

business expenses
circular flow
conglomerate
consumers
corporation
efficiency
expenditures
diminishing returns
diversification
first tragic flaw of capitalism
fixed inputs
horizontal expansion
households
incomes
increasing returns
law of diminishing returns

limited liability
lowest-cost technique
marginal physical product
neighborhood effect
partnership
productivity
purchasing power
sales
second tragic flaw of
    capitalism
single proprietorship
social cost
stage of production
unlimited liability
variable inputs
vertical expansion

COMPLETION QUESTIONS

Fill in the blanks with the proper word or words from the list above. Not all terms are used.

1. The additional contribution to production by an additional input is called the _____.

2. Because the second unit of labor increased output per worker, we can say that we are in a stage of _____.

3. The _____ is that in the great efficiency drive to lower the costs of production, we have provided the temptation to pollute.

4. The most simple form of business organization is a(n) _____.

5. Through _____, a firm takes over another stage of production.

6. _____ involve(s) doing more and more of the same type of operation.

7. The _____ applies when there is at least one fixed input for production.

8. From the business point of view, dollars paid to the resource markets are called _____.

9. The dollars that flow out of the households into the markets for goods and services are called consumer _____.

10. When pollution costs are passed on to society at large, there is a(n) _____.

11. The _____ is the tendency to be cold and unresponsive in the absence of purchasing power no matter what the basic need may be.

CROSSWORD PUZZLE

Fill in the crossword puzzle from the list of Important Terms and Concepts. Not all terms are used.

ACROSS
1. Those who have a direct demand for final goods and services.
5. Economist's measure of output gained per unit of input.
6. Choosing the lowest-cost technique.
8. Amounts purchased times their prices.
9. Has advantage of limited liability.
10. Type of business organization with shared duties.

DOWN
1. Primary advantage is diversification.
2. Results in revenue for the firm.
3. Supply resources to firms and act as consumers.
4. Producing several different products in a firm.
7. Dollars received by households for resources owned.

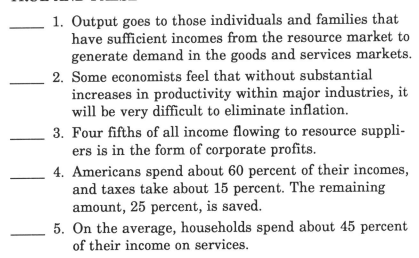

TRUE AND FALSE

_____ 1. Output goes to those individuals and families that have sufficient incomes from the resource market to generate demand in the goods and services markets.

_____ 2. Some economists feel that without substantial increases in productivity within major industries, it will be very difficult to eliminate inflation.

_____ 3. Four fifths of all income flowing to resource suppliers is in the form of corporate profits.

_____ 4. Americans spend about 60 percent of their incomes, and taxes take about 15 percent. The remaining amount, 25 percent, is saved.

_____ 5. On the average, households spend about 45 percent of their income on services.

_____ 6. The most direct way to approach the pollution problem would be to regulate; i.e., to state maximum levels of allowable pollution.

_____ 7. The drive to operate businesses at the lowest possible cost has contributed to pollution problems in the United States.

_____ 8. The reason the law of diminishing returns holds is that we assume that all inputs are not equally efficient.

_____ 9. A firm should keep hiring people as long as the value of the additional product of labor is less than the extra wages paid to get that product.

_____10. Partnerships dominate the mainstream of American business.

MULTIPLE CHOICE

1. Which of the following are types of business organizations according to the legal system?

   a. proprietorship, partnership, and corporation
   b. monopoly, pure competition, and oligopoly
   c. retail, wholesale, and service
   d. primary, secondary, and tertiary
   e. none of the above

2. The advantages of the corporate form of business is(are)

   a. ease of obtaining financial capital
   b. limited liability
   c. tax advantages
   d. all of the above
   e. none of the above

3. Diversification is the major advantage of

   a. proprietorships
   b. conglomerates
   c. partnerships
   d. corporations
   e. all of the above

4. If the owner of a gasoline station in a town bought up all the gasoline stations in that town, this would be an example of
   a. vertical expansion
   b. internal growth
   c. horizontal expansion
   d. conglomeration
   e. diversification

5. If the owner of a furniture store bought a lumber mill that supplied the store with wood, this would be an example of
   a. horizontal expansion
   b. internal growth
   c. conglomeration
   d. merger
   e. vertical expansion

6. A single proprietorship has the major advantage of
   a. limited liability
   b. tax advantages
   c. a minimum of red tape
   d. ease of gathering financial capital
   e. all of the above

7. Three out of five businesses fail before the third year of operation. How many million American businesses are there?
   a. 3
   b. 6
   c. 9
   d. 20
   e. 50

8. As supply and demand operate, what type of flows are found?
   a. money and income only
   b. goods and services only
   c. resources only
   d. money in one direction and real things in the other
   e. none of the above

9. The sales of businesses are viewed as what by the households?

   a. consumer expenditures
   b. income
   c. cost of production
   d. business receipts
   e. wages and salaries

10. The income of households is viewed as what by businesses?
   a. sales
   b. receipts
   c. consumer expenditures
   d. revenues
   e. business expenses

PROBLEMS AND DISCUSSION

1. Given that the yearly extra value contributed to production by Mr. Keller is $20,000, what is the maximum annual salary that he should be paid? What is the general rule that applies in such cases?

2. In the following figure show what would happen to the supply curve if a firm were forced to bear the cost of a pollution cleanup.

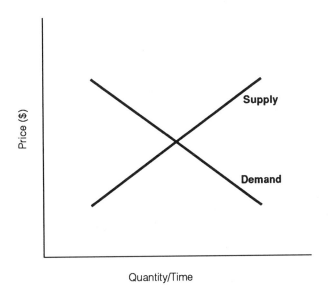

Quantity/Time

a. Is the new price higher? lower?

b. Is the quantity greater or smaller than before?

3. Efficiency was defined in this chapter as the least-cost method of production. What is the major limitation of this analysis as presented?

Chapter 4
ANSWERS

COMPLETION QUESTIONS

1. marginal physical product
2. increasing returns
3. first tragic flaw of capitalism
4. single proprietorship
5. vertical expansion
6. horizontal expansion

7. law of diminishing returns
8. business expenses
9. expenditures
10. neighborhood effect
11. second tragic flaw of capitalism

CROSSWORD PUZZLE

```
C O N S U M E R S
O     A
N     L             H         D
G     E             O         I
L     S     P R O D U C T I V I T Y
O                   S         E
M                   E         R
E F F I C I E N C Y H         S
R                   O         I
A                   L         F
T         I         D         I
E X P E N D I T U R E S       C
          C                   A
C O R P O R A T I O N         T
          M                   I
P A R T N E R S H I P         O
          S                   N
```

TRUE AND FALSE

1. true	6. true
2. true	7. true
3. false	8. false
4. false	9. false
5. true	10. false

MULTIPLE CHOICE

1. a	6. c
2. d	7. d
3. b	8. d
4. c	9. a
5. e	10. e

PROBLEMS AND DISCUSSION

1. The maximum salary Keller should receive for one year is $20,000. The general rule is to keep hiring people as long as the value of the additional product produced by labor is greater than the extra wages paid to obtain that product.

2. a. higher
   b. smaller

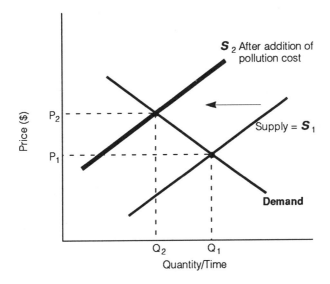

3. The major limitation of the least-cost method of production analysis presented in this chapter is that the method applies to a fixed amount of production that can be produced in alternative ways. If we need to consider various amounts of production compared to one another, then we will need to calculate average cost figures.

Chapter 5

GOVERNMENT

IMPORTANT TERMS AND CONCEPTS

ability-to-pay philosophy
benefits-received philosophy
big brother
business cycle
corporate income tax
entitlements
excise taxes
income redistribution
loopholes
mixed-capitalism
payroll tax

personal income tax
progressive tax
property tax
public goods
regressive tax
rules of the game
sales tax
second tragic flaw of
   capitalism
tax-free municipal bonds
third tragic flaw of
   capitalism

COMPLETION QUESTIONS

Fill in the blanks with the proper word or words from the list above. Not all terms are used.

1. _____ programs include welfare, public health, and Medicare.

2. Examples of the _____ include defining the legal responsibilities of business operations, enforcement of contracts, and defining property rights.

3. The government as the ultimate "overseer" of our activities is known as _____.

4. The _____ is(are) that there is no self-correcting mechanism to automatically pull the economy out of a severe slump.

5. The largest single area of federal spending is for _____.

6. The _____ contribute(s) over half of the revenues for state government.

7. Local governments derive almost half of their tax revenues from the _____.

8. Local governments use _____ as a method of borrowing.

9. A(n) _____ will result in more tax savings for a rich person than a poor person.

10. The _____, _____, and _____ are the three main sources of federal tax revenue.

CROSSWORD PUZZLE

Fill in the crossword puzzle from the list of Important Terms and Concepts. Not all terms are used.

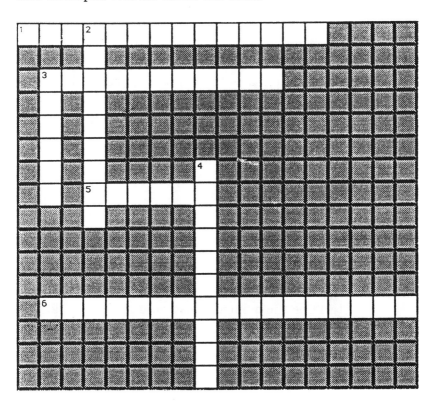

ACROSS

1. Philosophy of taxation based on income or wealth.
3. Tax that takes larger percentage as income increases.
5. Tax on goods like cigarettes.
6. Philosophy based on the use of a good or service.

DOWN

2. Legal means of lowering tax liability.
3. Goods that are usually unprofitable.
4. Tax that takes a larger percentage from the poor than rich.

TRUE AND FALSE

_____ 1. With a regressive tax, the poor pay a lower percent of their income than the rich.

_____ 2. The percentage of GNP accounted for by government spending has been rising for most of the last thirty years.

_____ 3. Most pollution laws need to be national in scope in order to be effective.

_____ 4. One economic function of government is to care for a special group of people—the economic failures and rejects.

_____ 5. The government should never attempt to maintain competition in the economy.

_____ 6. The government engages in unfair competition when it provides public goods.

_____ 7. The necessities of a civilized society are best provided with a public commitment to financing.

_____ 8. Economists, with their tools of analysis, can help determine the economic costs and benefits of different actions and policies.

_____ 9. The government should never attempt to make corrections to the ups and downs of the business cycle.

_____ 10. If the government destroys some freedoms, it enhances others.

MULTIPLE CHOICE

1. The major source of federal tax revenues is
   a. personal income tax
   b. sales tax
   c. property tax
   d. excise tax
   e. corporate income tax

2. The federal government spends most of its tax revenues on
   a. education
   b. defense
   c. entitlements
   d. interest on the national debt
   e. veterans' benefits

3. The states gather most of their tax revenues from
   a. property taxes
   b. licenses, permits, and fees
   c. excise taxes
   d. sales taxes
   e. none of the above

4. Local governments derive almost half of their revenues from the
   a. sales tax
   b. excise tax
   c. income tax
   d. federal government
   e. property tax

5. "He who pays the tax ought to get the benefits from the expenditures of that tax." This is the
   a. ability-to-pay philosophy
   b. benefits-received philosophy
   c. ethical philosophy
   d. egalitarian philosophy
   e. Marxian philosophy

6. "He who has more financial resources should pay more tax." This is the

    a. ethical philosophy
    b. religious philosophy
    c. moral philosophy
    d. ability-to-pay philosophy
    e. benefits-received philosophy

7. Hobby farms are an example of a(n)

    a. tax evasion
    b. tax loophole
    c. illegal activity
    d. all of the above
    e. none of the above

8. Generally, most economists feel that a(n) _____-type income tax is a fairer way to raise government revenue than a sales tax.

    a. regressive
    b. proportional
    c. flat-rate
    d. even
    e. progressive

9. The government enforces the "rules of the game" including

    a. providing the money supply
    b. providing for national defense
    c. regulating pollution
    d. regulating food and drugs
    e. providing highways

PROBLEMS AND DISCUSSION

1. Give the following table of information, answer questions a and b below.

Item	Individual	
	#1	#2
Income	$1,000	$5,000
Value of good purchased	$100	$100
Tax rate	6%	6%
Tax paid	$6	$6

a. What is the average tax (tax paid/income) for each individual?

b. Is this tax progressive or regressive? Why?

2. How can the government help correct the "third tragic flaw of capitalism"?

3. What functions of government would the most antigovernmental philosopher agree must be performed by government?

4. "While there is a division of responsibility among federal, state and local governments, certain revenue sources may be best suited to national collection." Explain this statement.

Chapter 5
ANSWERS

COMPLETION QUESTIONS

1. income redistribution
2. rules of the game
3. big brother
4. third tragic flaw of capitalism
5. entitlements
6. sales tax
7. property tax
8. tax-free municipal bonds
9. regressive tax
10. payroll tax, personal income tax, corporate income tax

CROSSWORD PUZZLE

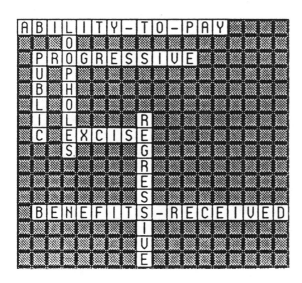

TRUE AND FALSE

1. false	6. false
2. true	7. true
3. true	8. true
4. true	9. false
5. false	10. true

MULTIPLE CHOICE

1. a	6. d
2. c	7. b
3. d	8. e
4. e	9. d
5. b	

PROBLEMS AND DISCUSSION

1. a. For individual #1 the average tax is $6/$1,000 = .006 or 0.6 percent.
   For individual #2 the average tax is $6/$5,000 = .0012 or 0.12 percent.

   b. The tax is regressive, because the average tax falls as income increases.

2. The "third tragic flaw of capitalism" is that there is no automatic self-correcting mechanism to pull the economy out of a recession. The government could use fiscal and monetary policies to stimulate the economy during these periods.

3. The most antigovernmental philosopher would say that the government should at a minimum provide a money supply, national defense, and a system of law and order.

4. The concept of division of responsibility refers to specific areas of responsibility being traditionally allocated to different levels of government. For example, national defense is the responsibility of the federal government; education and highways are the responsibility of the state government; and police and fire protection are the responsibility of local governments. The size of the bureaucracy necessary to handle the collection and auditing of certain taxes, such as the

income tax or the social security tax, preclude their being collected on the state or local level. If a state or local government were to have, for example, an income tax, there would need to be much consideration given to the cost of the bureaucracy necessary to collect and police it.

Chapter 6

POVERTY

IMPORTANT TERMS AND CONCEPTS

Aid to Families with Dependent Children (AFDC)
feminization of poverty
Food Stamp program
income floor
invisible
Medicaid
negative income tax
single-parent households
Social Security

structurally unemployed
transfer payments
underclass
unemployment compen-
  sation
veterans' benefits
vicious economic circle
welfare recipients
white-collar occupation
workfare

COMPLETION QUESTIONS

Fill in the blanks with the proper word or words from the list
above. Not all terms are used.

1. _____ is a welfare program designed for children and their mothers who do not have another adult
   as part of the family unit.

2. The _____ are people who find themselves out
   of work even though the economy may be booming.

3. Some impoverished are trapped by the _____.

4. _____, _____ , and _____
   are all considered transfer payments, although they are
   paid to people in all income groups.

5. Another form of help from the government is goods and
   services in lieu of cash. An example of this type of help
   for food is the _____.

6. The idea for the _____ originated with Milton
   Friedman in his book *Capitalism and Freedom.*

7. _____ requires that able-bodied welfare
   recipients accept public service or private employment.

8. Approximately 90% of _____ are headed by
   the mother.

CROSSWORD PUZZLE

Fill in the crossword puzzle from the list of Important Terms and Concepts. Not all terms are used.

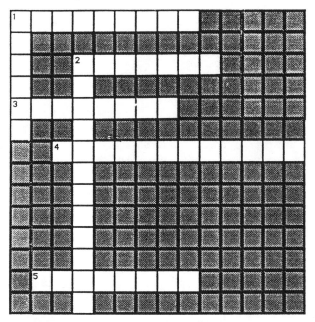

ACROSS

1. Michael Harrington's term for the poor.
2. Recipients are usually children.
3. A medical program for the poor.
4. Referring to poverty of so many single-parent families.
5. Payments flow from the government to individuals.

DOWN

1. A major feature of a negative income tax is a guaranteed _____.
2. Occupations result in above average incomes.

TRUE AND FALSE

_____ 1. The negative income tax system would be more expensive than the present system.

_____ 2. The negative income tax system would still be as humiliating and dehumanizing as the present system.

_____ 3. With the negative income tax system a person would normally receive 100 percent of his or her unused exemptions and deductions.

_____ 4. The incentive to work would be maintained with the negative income tax system.

_____ 5. Our present welfare system has the unintended effect of encouraging the breakup of families.

_____ 6. Welfare always satisfies the basic economic needs of the people.

_____ 7. Once on welfare, always on welfare.

_____ 8. Welfare families are getting rich and "living it up."

_____ 9. Many poor people lack internal vitality because of repeated failures.

_____10. Approximately 15 percent of the aged have incomes that fall below the poverty lines.

MULTIPLE CHOICE

1. According to Michael Harrington, the poor are
   a. economically invisible
   b. politically invisible
   c. without internal vitality
   d. all of the above
   e. none of the above

2. Structural unemployment is caused by
   a. out-of-date skills
   b. the business cycle
   c. laziness
   d. the minimum wage
   e. all of the above

3. Nonwhites
   a. have the same average incomes as whites
   b. have unemployment that is at least double that of whites
   c. finish high school just as often as whites
   d. have as many white-collar jobs as whites
   e. none of the above

4. Poverty is basically an economic problem that needs economic solutions. The poor need
   a. jobs
   b. income
   c. retraining for current skills
   d. mobility
   e. all of the above

5. A transfer payment is
   a. a payment for a good or service
   b. a payment for a resource
   c. a flow of money for which nothing is expected in return
   d. a credit changed to a debit
   e. a circular-flow concept

6. Most economists feel that the present-day welfare system is
   a. poorly designed
   b. inefficient
   c. expensive
   d. all of the above
   e. none of the above

7. What is everyone allowed to subtract from their gross income before figuring personal income taxes?
   a. cost and revenues
   b. exemptions and deductions
   c. profits and sales
   d. debits and credits
   e. stocks and flows

8. The negative income tax is, in essence, a

    a. guaranteed income plan
    b. jobs program
    c. job-training program
    d. regressive tax system
    e. proportional tax system

9. The advantages of the negative tax system include

    a. only special coverage
    b. no need for the present system to be changed
    c. its being designed so that it would not discourage work
    d. all of the above
    e. none of the above

10. More than _____ million men, women, and children are unable to successfully participate in our competitive capitalist system.

    a. 5
    b. 10
    c. 15
    d. 20
    e. 30

PROBLEMS AND DISCUSSION

1. Given that Miss Ozmun has earned $1,000, that she has exemptions and deductions of $4,000, and that the negative income tax rate is 0.5, what would be the answers to the following:

    a. the size of the negative income tax transfer payment

    b. Miss Ozmun's total income

2. List the negative features of today's welfare system.

3. Why is it difficult to identify the poverty line?

4. What are the major factors that account for the concept of "the feminization of poverty"?

Chapter 6
ANSWERS

COMPLETION QUESTIONS

1. Aid to Families with Dependent Children (AFDC)
2. structurally unemployed
3. vicious economic circle
4. Social Security, unemployment compensation, veterans' benefits
5. Food Stamp program
6. negative income tax
7. workfare
8. single-parent households

CROSSWORD PUZZLE

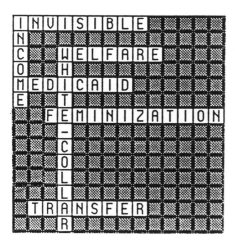

TRUE AND FALSE

1. true	6. false
2. false	7. false
3. false	8. false
4. true	9. true
5. true	10. true

MULTIPLE CHOICE

1. d	6. d
2. a	7. b
3. b	8. a
4. e	9. c
5. c	10. e

PROBLEMS AND DISCUSSION

1. a. $1,500
   b. $2,500

2. The negative features of the present welfare system include

   a. Welfare does not always satisfy the basic economic needs of the people.

   b. The welfare system is often inefficient.

   c. Welfare can be dehumanizing.

   d. Our present welfare system has the unintended effect of encouraging the breakup of families.

3. Poverty can be measured in absolute and relative senses. Within one society, a group in relative poverty might be well off compared to groups in other societies. This means that it is very difficult to compare poverty in different societies. Even within a single society the definition of absolute poverty is arbitrary, subject to change, and influenced by the standard of living in that society.

4. The feminization of poverty is accounted for by the increase in divorce rates and numbers of unwed mothers as well as the fact that approximately 90 percent of single parent households are headed by females.

Chapter 7

MACROECONOMICS

IMPORTANT TERMS AND CONCEPTS

base year	macroeconomics
composition	money GDP
density commodities	nonmarket transactions
disinflation	price index
economic wealth	quality
gross domestic product (GDP)	real GDP
inflation	real growth

COMPLETION QUESTIONS

Fill in the blanks with the proper word or words from the list above. Not all terms are used.

1. _____ measure(s) the value of all the buildings and structures, equipment inventories, and other natural resources at a certain point in time.

2. The _____ is a measure of the final total value of all goods and services produced within a nation's borders over a year's time.

3. Distorted or inflated GDP is called _____.

4. Economist Leopold Kohr has defined _____ as those goods purchased by consumers, governments, and business to simply offset the impact of living in a high-density environment and among large-scale social institutions.

5. _____ is money GDP adjusted for price changes.

6. The _____ for the base year is always equal to 100.

7. _____ is when real per capita GDP increases.

8. _____ include(s) do-it-yourself projects.

CROSSWORD PUZZLE

Fill in the crossword puzzle from the list of Important Terms and Concepts. All terms are not used.

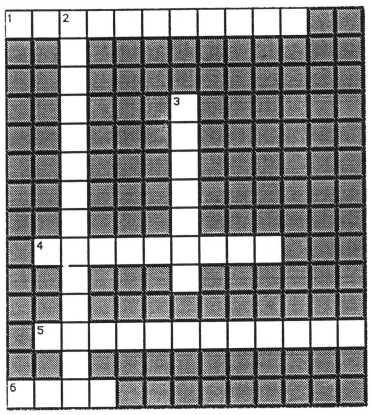

ACROSS

1. Is just as important in GDP as individual goods.
4. Distorts GDP calculations when prices increase.
5. When inflation increases at decreasing rates.
6. Year used to compare each year's output and prices.

DOWN

2. The study of broad concepts of an economic system.
3. Changes make it difficult to define a product.

TRUE AND FALSE

_____ 1. There was a period of real economic growth from the early 1940s to the late 1960s.

_____ 2. Change in a price index compared with the price index for the base year records percentage change.

_____ 3. All changes in money GDP are due to price changes.

_____ 4. Happiness is rising GDP.

_____ 5. Environmentalists are distressed by the ugliness of overdevelopment.

_____ 6. Progrowth people point out that cleaning up the environment will be expensive and that the additional resources must come from somewhere.

_____ 7. According to Irving Kristol's argument, growth is not necessarily a precondition to a modern democracy.

_____ 8. Headache remedies are an example of a density commodity.

_____ 9. There are economic "bads" as well as "goods."

MULTIPLE CHOICE

1. If output rises by 3 percent and population goes up 1 percent, then the average family will
   a. suffer a decline of 2 percent in its standard of living
   b. suffer a decline of 4 percent in its standard of living
   c. will enjoy a 2 percent increase in its standard of living
   d. will have a constant standard of living
   e. none of the above

2. At the beginning of the 1980s the total money GDP in the United States was approximately how many dollars?
   a. 1 billion
   b. 1 trillion
   c. 100 trillion
   d. 100 billion
   e. 3 trillion

3. Economic wealth is a "stock" concept: GDP is a(n)

   a. flow
   b. stock
   c. unknown
   d. exogenous variable
   e. all of the above

4. Public officials are interested in macroeconomics because

   a. they are oracles
   b. they directly or indirectly accept the responsibility for maintaining the economic health of the country
   c. they are "futurists"
   d. they are economic soothsayers
   e. none of the above

5. "You could very well have stopped growing after the First World War. There was enough technology to make life quite pleasant. Cities weren't overgrown." This is the position of

   a. Irving Kristol
   b. John Kenneth Galbraith
   c. Leopold Kohr
   d. Ezra Mishan
   e. E. B. White

6. "Man almost literally made the cow, the fat corn kernel, the plump turkey, the beautiful rose . . . he still made the world enormously better." This is the position of

   a. Author Mel Ellis, a naturalist
   b. Ezra Mishan
   c. John Kenneth Galbraith
   d. Milton Friedman
   e. none of the above

7. The idea "Happiness is a rising GDP" is challenged by what factors?

   a. inflation
   b. pollution
   c. density commodities
   d. all of the above
   e. none of the above

8. The price index for the base year is always

   a. 1
   b. 50
   c. 1,000
   d. unknown
   e. 100

9. Money GDP is best deflated with the

   a. CPI
   b. GDP price deflator
   c. PPI
   d. escalator clause
   e. none of the above

10. The decade of the 1960s saw what percentage of real growth per year?

   a. 0
   b. 10
   c. 4.5
   d. 100
   e. 2

PROBLEMS AND DISCUSSION

1. Given the following data:

   1992 money GDP = $1,528.80
   1992 price index (1985 base) = 125.6

Adjusting for 1985 prices, what was real GDP in 1992?

2. Define "density commodities" and give a list of several examples of this type of good.

3. "The government is clearly a 'winner' when inflation occurs. Therefore, the government should not work to keep inflation from occurring, but should make sure that inflation does occur." Critically evaluate this statement.

4. What happens to real GDP when disinflation occurs?

Chapter 7
ANSWERS

COMPLETION QUESTIONS

1. economic wealth
2. gross domestic product (GDP)
3. money GDP
4. density commodities
5. real GDP
6. price index
7. real growth
8. nonmarket transactions

CROSSWORD PUZZLE

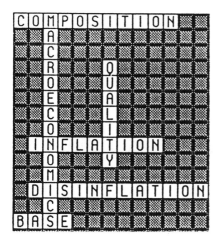

TRUE AND FALSE

1. true	6. true
2. true	7. false
3. false	8. true
4. false	9. true
5. true	

MULTIPLE CHOICE

1. c	6. a
2. e	7. d
3. a	8. e
4. b	9. b
5. d	10. c

PROBLEMS AND DISCUSSION

1

$$1992 \text{ real GDP} = \frac{1992 \text{ money GDP}}{\text{price index } 1985} \times 100 = \frac{\$1,528.80}{125.6} \times 100 = \$1,217$$

2. According to British economist Leopold Kohr, density commodities are those goods that are purchased to offset the impact of living in a high-density environment and among large-scale institutions. Examples of this type of good or service include the cost of traffic accidents, many legal services, commuting expenses, escapist media, chemical relaxants and stimulants, and crime.

3. The government can be called a "winner" from the perspective that it receives increased tax revenues without having to legislate a tax increase. This is due to the progressive tax system. When inflation occurs, most wages and salaries increase. The higher incomes received by workers push them into higher tax brackets and their income is taxed at a higher marginal rate. On the other hand, because the poor and those on fixed incomes are hurt by inflation and because both income and GDP are distorted, governments should discourage inflation. The damage to society as a whole caused by high inflation is too great for governments to tolerate.

4. Disinflation occurs when the rate of inflation declines from year to year. As long as inflation occurs, real GDP is less than its associated money GDP; thus, periods of disinflation are characterized as calculations of real GDP that are higher than they would be if inflation were increasing at increasing rates.

Chapter 8

UNEMPLOYMENT AND INFLATION

IMPORTANT TERMS AND CONCEPTS

classical economists
consumption (C)
cost-push inflation
deficit
demand-pull inflation
depression
discouraged workers
fiscal policy
flexible incomes
frictional unemployment
fully employed
government expenditures (G)
Great Depression
hyperinflation
investment (I)
Keynesian unemployment
lenders
multiplier effect

net foreign exports (X_n)
Phillips curve
public debt
output = employment
recession
savers
saving
Say's Law
speculator
spending
stagflation
structurally unemployed
supply-side economic theory
surplus
total demand
total income = GDP
total supply
unemployment

COMPLETION QUESTIONS

Fill in the blanks with the proper word or words from the list above. Not all terms are used.

1. During the _____ there was as much as 25 percent unemployment.

2. When _____ is equal to _____ there is equilibrium.

3. The act of not spending is called _____.

4. Because for every dollar's worth of output there will be also a dollar's worth of income generated, we can say that _____.

5. Inflation that is the result of higher costs is often referred to as _____.

6. When extra demand causes prices to rise, it is called _____.

7. If output is high, we know employment will also be high and vice versa; therefore, we can say_____.

8. People with _____ do fairly well during inflationary times.

9. There is(are) _____ when a resource is idle.

10. _____ result(s) from those people who are looking for a job for the first time or changing jobs voluntarily.

11. The economy is _____ when there is still 4 percent unemployment.

12. The _____ is(are) workers whose skills have become obsolete.

13. _____ result(s) from a lack of spending.

14. _____ state(s) that "supply creates its own demand."

15. _____, _____, _____, and _____ are the four major categories of spending.

16. The two budgetary policies of spending and taxation make up what is known as _____.

17. The _____ reflect(s) the fact that a relatively small increase in spending results in a large increase in output and income.

18. _____ revolve(s) around two key ideas: economic incentives and economic growth.

CROSSWORD PUZZLE

Fill in the crossword puzzle from the list of Important Terms and Concepts. Not all terms are used.

ACROSS

1. Those who earn interest.
5. Curve shows tradeoff of inflation; unemployment of inflation.
7. The bottom of the business cycle.
8. Those who are paid interest on demand deposits.
10. Economists who call long-term unemployment impossible.
12. Workers stop looking for employment.
13. Runaway inflation.

DOWN

2. A budget with a negative balance.
3. Purchases assets to take advantage.
4. Purchases that sum to total demand.
6. A budget with a positive balance.
9. When the rate of growth of GDP is first negative.
11. Stagnation plus inflation.

TRUE AND FALSE

_____ 1. Supply-side recommendations include generous tax credits for business investment.

_____ 2. The economists' recommendations to increase taxes and to cut spending during inflation are usually "enjoyable" for a politician.

_____ 3. The correct anti-inflationary policy would be to raise taxes, lower government spending, and generally work toward a budgetary surplus.

_____ 4. There is no reason why the multiplier effect would not work in reverse.

_____ 5. A relatively large increase in spending results in a relatively small increase in output and income.

_____ 6. John M. Keynes's great discovery was that an economic system might be in a stable equilibrium at a depression level of GDP.

_____ 7. For every dollar's worth of output there will be a dollar's worth of income generated.

_____ 8. Every point on the 45-degree line represents a greater value on the vertical axis than on the horizontal axis.

_____ 9. There is a level of output so low that savings might be negative.

_____ 10. The classical economists would say "stay cool and everything will take care of itself."

MULTIPLE CHOICE

1. Keynesian unemployment is due to
    a. lack of spending
    b. obsolete jobs
    c. voluntary job change
    d. looking for a first job
    e. none of the above

2. When the economy is fully employed there is still what percentage of the population without work?

   a. 10
   b. 4
   c. 0
   d. 50
   e. 100

3. Frictional unemployment is due to

   a. a lack of spending
   b. the business cycle
   c. those looking for work for the first time or those voluntarily changing jobs
   d. obsolete skills
   e. all of the above

4. Structural unemployment is due to

   a. the business cycle
   b. looking for a first job
   c. voluntarily changing jobs
   d. obsolete skills
   e. the minimum wage

5. Those hurt by inflation include

   a. those on flexible incomes
   b. labor unions with escalator clauses
   c. large corporations
   d. speculators
   e. savers

6. Inflation is bad because it

   a. distorts the economy
   b. redistributes income from one group to another
   c. hurts people on fixed incomes
   d. all of the above
   e. none of the above

7. Phase III has what effect on prices, employment, and output?

   a. No increase in prices; employment and output increase.
   b. All three increase.
   c. Prices increase; employment and output cannot.
   d. All three elements fall.
   e. Prices fall; unemployment and output increase.

8. Demand-pull inflation is due to

   a. too much spending
   b. labor cost increases
   c. energy cost increases
   d. minimum wage laws
   e. monopoly power

9. Once there is upward motion in the economy, everything tends to reinforce the trend. As a result,

   a. prices tend to fall
   b. greater spending generates more employment, income, and investment spending
   c. less spending reinforces the negative multiplier effect
   d. all of the above
   e. none of the above

10. The inability of pure capitalism to regulate itself is

   a. Marxism
   b. socialism
   c. capitalism's first tragic flaw
   d. capitalism's second tragic flaw
   e. capitalism's third tragic flaw

PROBLEMS AND DISCUSSION

1. Use the following figure to illustrate Keynes's prescriptions to bring the economy to full employment.

   a. What two policy changes could bring about the change you've indicated?

b. What is likely to happen to the budget under these conditions?

2. What were the major parts of the classical theory?

3. "If people became less thrifty, the level of output and income could rise." Explain this statement.

4. How could a decrease in thriftiness be detrimental to the economy?

COMPLETION QUESTIONS

1. Great Depression
2. total supply, total demand
3. saving
4. total income = GDP
5. cost-push inflation
6. demand-pull inflation
7. output = employment
8. flexible incomes
9. unemployment
10. frictional unemployment
11. fully employed
12. structurally unemployed
13. Keynesian unemployment
14. Say's Law
15. consumption, investment, government expenditure, and net foreign exports
16. fiscal policy
17. multiplier effect
18. supply-side economic theory

CROSSWORD PUZZLE

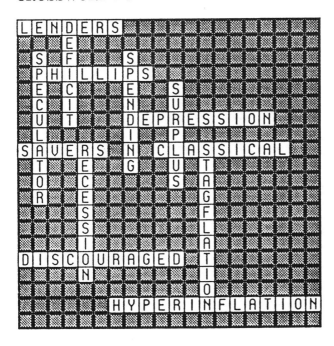

TRUE AND FALSE

1. true	6. true
2. false	7. true
3. true	8. false
4. true	9. true
5. false	10. true

MULTIPLE CHOICE

1. a	6. d
2. b	7. c
3. c	8. a
4. d	9. b
5. e	10. e

PROBLEMS AND DISCUSSION

1.

a. decrease taxes and increase government spending
b. deficit

2. The major features of the classical theory were (a) Say's Law—supply creates its own demand, (b) prices and wages flex downward (c) involuntary unemployment is impossible in the long run, and (d) the system is self-correcting.

3. Income can either be spent or saved. If people become less thrifty, they will attempt to save less and spend more out of any given level of income. As they spend more, the consumption function shifts upward to the left and the equilibrium level of output and income moves to a higher level. At a higher level of output, businesses will need more workers, so the level of employment increases also.

4. A decrease in thriftiness could lead to a decrease in saving. If saving decreases, there will be less money available for businesses to borrow to finance investment projects. Business investment today leads to increased output and employment for the future. If business investment is retarded because of a lack of funds, future output and employment will be reduced.

Chapter 9

MONEY

IMPORTANT TERMS AND CONCEPTS

banker's banks
barter
commodity money
currency
demand deposits
discount rate
discounts
discretionary monetary policy
divided and multiplied
durable
easily transferred
easy money conditions
excess reserves
Fed
fiat money
financial intermediary
fine-tuning

limited supply
manipulate credit controls
medium of exchange
member banks
monetarists
Monetary Rule
not easily duplicated illegally
open-market operations
pecuniary
reserve ratio
reserves
social trust
standard of value
store of value
thrift institutions
tight money conditions
token money

COMPLETION QUESTIONS

Fill in the blanks with the proper word or words from the list above. Not all terms are used.

1. Money functions as _____, _____, and _____.

2. The desirable attributes of money include:

    • It is _____.

    • It is _____ from place to place.

    • Its basic unit can be _____.

    • It is in _____.

    • It is _____.

3. In the United States _____ "back(s) up" the value of money.

4. Checking accounts are also known as _____.

5. The ratio of required reserve deposits to total demand deposits is known as the _____.

6. Reserves beyond what is required by the Fed are known as _____.

7. _____ are called for when the economy is in recession.

8. _____ are called for when the economy is inflated.

9. The commercial banks that hold stock in the Fed are called _____.

10. The middleman between savers and investors is called a(n) _____.

11. The regional Fed banks function as _____; i.e., they hold deposits and make loans to member banks.

12. The interest rate charged by the Fed for loaning reserves to member banks is called the _____.

13. _____ include(s) the buying and selling of government securities.

CROSSWORD PUZZLE

Fill in the crossword puzzle from the list of Important Terms and Concepts. Not all terms are used.

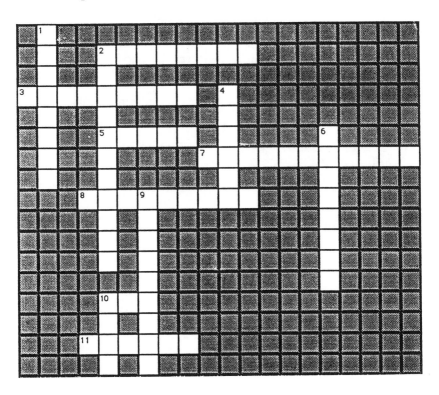

ACROSS
  2. Rule is to increase money supply at constant rate.
  3. Referring to money matters.
  5. Money has metal content worth less than face value
  7. When the Fed makes small loans adjustment to policy.
  8. Loans made by Fed to member banks.
  10. Federal Reserve System.
  11. Direct exchange without use of money.

DOWN
1. Deposits of member banks in the Fed.
2. They believe that fine-tuning causes problems.
4. Institutions that include saving and loans.
6. Paper money and coins.
9. Money that has intrinsic worth in form of a good.
10. Money that is declared by government to have value.

TRUE AND FALSE

_____ 1. It is impossible for an economy to operate without money.

_____ 2. The function of money as a "store of value" means money acts as a common denominator.

_____ 3. We must be able to expand the amount of money in the economy as the economy itself expands.

_____ 4. The value of money in the United States is backed up by the precious metals of gold and silver.

_____ 5. We need to have just the right balance between output and money in order for our dollars to remain valuable.

_____ 6. Money is valuable because we have faith that each one of us will accept it as a legitimate medium of exchange.

_____ 7. Money must be printed on paper or stamped out of metal.

_____ 8. The money supply is controlled by monetary regulations and controls.

_____ 9. The 20-man Board of Governors at the Fed oversees the 30 regional Fed banks.

_____10. All banks are required to join the Fed.

MULTIPLE CHOICE

1. An example of a financial intermediary is
   a. a stock broker
   b. an investment broker
   c. an insurance firm
   d. the government
   e. a commercial bank

2. The loans that the Fed makes to member banks are known as

a. reserves
b. deposits
c. transfers
d. discounts
e. none of the above

3. Excess reserves limit the amount of _____ a bank can make.

a. deposits
b. investments
c. loans
d. demand deposits
e. all of the above

4. Power over the reserve ratio is translated into power over the

a. money supply
b. buying and selling of government securities
c. interest charged to borrow reserves
d. all of the above
e. none of the above

5. Who is in charge of the buying and selling of government securities by the Fed?

a. the President
b. the local banker
c. the Open Market Committee
d. the Congress
e. none of the above

6. What is the link between changes in monetary policy and changes in spending in the economy?

a. discounts
b. reserves
c. the Congress
d. the interest rate
e. no link

7. If the society were facing severe inflation, then the action taken by the Fed would be

   a. to raise the reserve ratios
   b. to lower the discount rate
   c. to buy government securities
   d. all of the above
   e. none of the above

8. For recession, the appropriate monetary policies for easing credit conditions would be

   a. to raise the reserve ratio
   b. to buy government securities
   c. to raise the discount rate
   d. all of the above
   e. none of the above

9. Economists feel that monetary policy works best for

   a. supply and demand
   b. recession
   c. depression
   d. consumption
   e. inflation

PROBLEMS AND DISCUSSION

1. Construct a figure like the one below to show Fed monetary policy appropriate for recession.

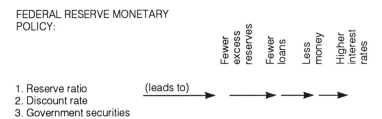

FEDERAL RESERVE MONETARY POLICY:

1. Reserve ratio
2. Discount rate
3. Government securities

(leads to) → Fewer excess reserves → Fewer loans → Less money → Higher interest rates

2. Construct a figure similar to **Figure 9-1** from the text (reproduced here) to illustrate what would happen if Fed policy were used to bring an economy out of a recession to full employment.

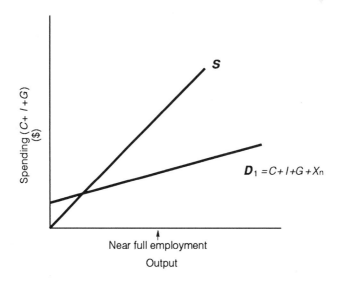

3. Explain how inflation tends to erode the "store of value" function of money.

4. "The only way to increase GDP through policies of the government is to use fiscal policy to fine-tune the economy." True or false? Explain.

Chapter 9
ANSWERS

COMPLETION QUESTIONS

1. medium of exchange, standard of value, store of value
2. durable, easily transferred, divided and multiplied, limited supply, not easily duplicated illegally
3. social trust
4. demand deposits
5. reserve ratio
6. excess reserves
7. easy money conditions
8. tight money conditions
9. member banks
10. financial intermediary
11. banker's banks
12. discount rate
13. open-market operations

CROSSWORD PUZZLE

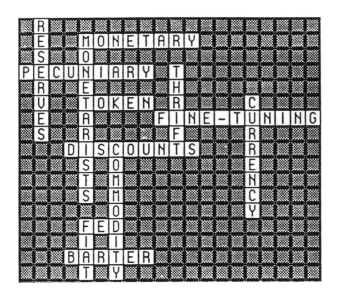

TRUE AND FALSE

1. false	6. true
2. false	7. false
3. true	8. true
4. false	9. false
5. true	10. false

MULTIPLE CHOICE

1. e	6. d
2. d	7. c
3. c	8. a
4. d	9. e
5. c	

PROBLEMS AND DISCUSSION

1.

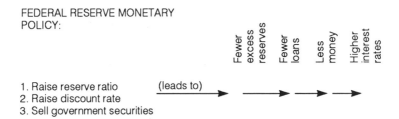

FEDERAL RESERVE MONETARY
POLICY:

| | Fewer excess reserves | Fewer loans | Less money | Higher interest rates |

1. Raise reserve ratio   (leads to) →
2. Raise discount rate   → → → →
3. Sell government securities

2.

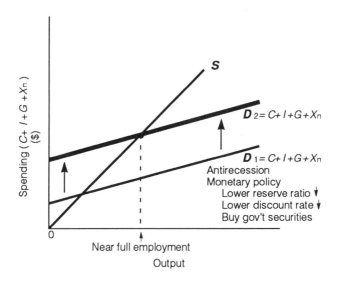

3. For money to safely and efficiently perform its function as a store of value, its value must be stable over time. People save money today to ensure the ability to take care of their needs in the future. But inflation erodes the purchasing power of savings and therefore creates an uncertainty as to the future purchasing power of money being saved today. When people lose confidence in the stability of money as protection against needs in the future, they will turn to other methods of storing wealth, such as real estate.

4. False. Monetary policy can also affect the level of GDP. The major mechanism is a several-step process that leads to a change in interest rates and in turn affects investment. In addition, other monetary policy changes (such as those shown in the answer to problem 1) can also have impacts on the GDP.

Chapter 10

THE BENEFITS OF TRADE

IMPORTANT TERMS AND CONCEPTS

absolute advantage
cheap foreign labor
comparative advantage
ethical grounds
expanded production-
   possibilities curve
General Agreement for
   Tariffs and Trade
global economy
infant industry argument
keep our money in the
   country
multinationals

mutual interdependence
nontariff barriers
North American Free Trade
   Agreement
opportunity costs
protectionism
quota
retaliate
tariff
theory of comparative
   advantage
trade-restriction war

COMPLETION QUESTIONS

Fill in the blanks with the proper word or words from the list above. Not all terms are used.

1. _____ has(have) been criticized for creating an "unhealthy dependence," especially on critical imports such as those related to defense.

2. The trade protectionism argument that we should _____ fails to recognize the "two-way street" feature of trade.

3. The trade protectionism argument concerning _____ fails to recognize differences in productivity between countries.

4. Even though one country might have an absolute advantage in all aspects of trade, the other countries will still have a(n) _____ in the trade of some items.

5. The gains from trade can be shown with a(n) _____.

6. _____ include(s) advertising campaigns that praise the virtues of domestically produced products.

7. David Ricardo developed the _____, which shows that trade is to the benefit of two countries even if one has a(n) _____.

8. The _____ of domestic trade versus foreign result(s) in gains being made from trade.

9. The _____ for protectionism may be used for short periods of time in developing countries.

10. The _____ have significantly lowered trade barriers since 1947.

11. The use of "cheap foreign labor" sometimes results in a(n) _____.

12. Trade agreements among the United States, Mexico, and Canada are outlined in the _____.

CROSSWORD PUZZLE

Fill in the crossword puzzle from the list of Important Terms and Concepts. Not all terms are used.

ACROSS
1. Firms with operations in more than one country.
3. To react to tariffs and quotas.
6. There are very few good reasons for ——.
7. The worldwide nature of competition.

DOWN
2. Tax-like barrier to trade.
4. Ground that may be used for protectionism.
5. Quantity barriers to trade.

TRUE AND FALSE

_____ 1. Protectionism may be used in traditional handicraft societies when there is a sudden, unexpected influx of machine-made goods.

_____ 2. There are no conditions that warrant interference with free trade.

_____ 3. With the cheap foreign labor argument, you usually discover an oblique admission that a particular industry is no longer efficient according to world standards.

_____ 4. If there is a healthy trade arrangement between countries, our money will eventually return to us.

_____ 5. A quota will make the demand curve for an import vertical at a particular quantity.

_____ 6. Although economists dislike protectionist measures in any guise, they dislike quotas most of all.

_____ 7. Protectionist measures usually do not hurt the consumer.

_____ 8. The greater the elasticity of demand, the more a tariff will help the domestic industry achieve its goal of keeping out foreign competition.

_____ 9. The economic effect of a tariff is the same as that of putting an exercise tax on any product.

_____10. Governments should not help displaced industries and workers hurt by foreign competition.

MULTIPLE CHOICE

1. One lesson of trade theory is that
   a. no one suffers from trade
   b. imported products will almost always bring some degree of economic suffering to those industries directly affected
   c. jobs in export industries will be lost
   d. all of the above
   e. none of the above

2. The first reaction to "cheap imports" is usually
   a. pressure for a political response
   b. call for nontariff barriers; i.e., advertising campaigns
   c. formation of powerful trade associations
   d. all of the above
   e. none of the above

3. Though certainly causing short-run dislocations, the net long-run effect will be _____ as each country pursues its comparative advantage.
   a. neutral
   b. unknown
   c. insignificant
   d. negative
   e. positive

4. The expanded production-possibilities curve is _____ the original one.
   a. right of
   b. left of
   c. the same as
   d. always steeper than
   e. always flatter than

5. A _____ curve can be used to illustrate the opportunity costs of compromises made because of trade.
   a. demand-supply
   b. cost-revenue
   c. production-possibilities
   d. profit-loss
   e. none of the above

6. If a country is more efficient in producing all goods, then it has a(n) _____.
   a. comparative advantage in the production of all goods
   b. absolute advantage
   c. free rider
   d. all of the above
   e. none of the above

7. Who developed the theory of comparative advantage?
   a. Adam Smith
   b. Milton Friedman
   c. John Kenneth Galbraith
   d. Jim Eggert
   e. David Ricardo

8. Trade provides
   a. an outlet for surpluses
   b. a way to get essential raw materials
   c. some healthy rivalry in certain industries
   d. neither a nor b
   e. a, b, and c are all true

9. International trade creates a sense of _____ among world nations and can have the side effect of enhancing world peace.

   a. interdependence
   b. independence
   c. nationalism
   d. all of the above
   e. none of the above

10. Perhaps the most obvious reason to trade is
    a. to keep our money at home
    b. to displace domestic workers
    c. to get essential raw materials
    d. to use cheap foreign labor
    e. none of the above

PROBLEMS AND DISCUSSION

1. Given the following data:

Domestic Trade-Off
Good X for Good Y

Country A	1 for 2
Country B	1 for 3

a. Which country has the absolute advantage in the production of good X?

b. Country _____ has a comparative advantage in the production of good X.

c. Country _____ has a comparative advantage in the production of good Y.

d. If fractions are allowed, then what is the likely compromise if trade takes place between country A and country B?

2. On the following figure illustrate the effect of a tariff placed on the import of good X.

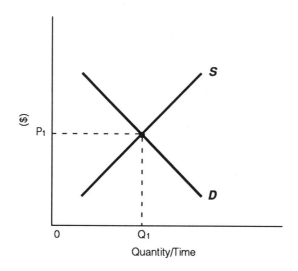

3. The market for videocassette recorders (VCRs) in the
   hypothetical country is shown in the following figure.
   Initially it does not engage in trade with other countries
   and the price of VCRs is $800 each as shown by the inter-
   section of demand (D) with domestic supply (S). Quantity
   exchanged equals Q.

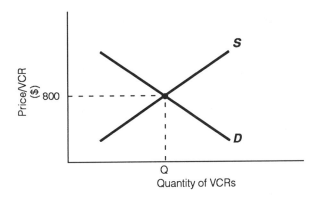

a. Show what would result if the country engaged in trade
   and the world price for VCRs was $300 each. Who would
   gain and lose relative to the situation prior to free
   trade?

b. Now suppose that the government decided to impose a
   tariff of $200 per unit on all imported VCRs, effectively
   raising the price in the market from $300 to $500 each.
   Use the figure to show the effect of this policy. Who are
   the gainers and losers relative to the free trade situation
   described in (a) above?

4. Identify the type of argument for protectionism found in
   the following quote. Why is it incorrect? "Tariffs and quotas
   should be placed on shoes made in Italy, because workers
   in America need a higher wage than workers in Italy."

Chapter 10
ANSWERS

COMPLETION QUESTIONS

1. mutual interdependence
2. keep our money in the country
3. cheap foreign labor
4. comparative advantage
5. expanded production-possibilities curve
6. nontariff barriers
7. theory of comparative advantage, absolute advantage
8. opportunity costs
9. infant industry argument
10. General Agreements for Tariffs and Trade
11. trade-restriction war
12. North American Free Trade Agreement

CROSSWORD PUZZLE

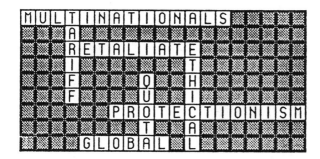

TRUE AND FALSE

1. true
2. false
3. true
4. true
5. false
6. true
7. false
8. true
9. true
10. false

MULTIPLE CHOICE

1. b
2. d
6. b
7. e

3. e   8. e
4. a   9. a
5. c   10. c

PROBLEMS AND DISCUSSION

1. a. country A
   b. A
   c. B
   d. 1 to 2 1/2

2.

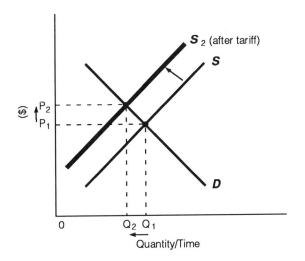

3.

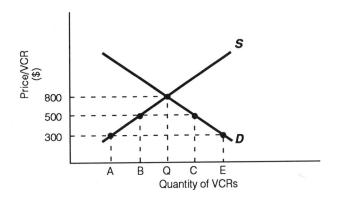

(a) Domestic consumption would increase by an amount
equal to QE units.
Domestic production would decrease by an amount
equal to AQ units.
Price would fall to $300, a decrease of $500.

Domestic consumers would gain by having more VCRs
at a lower price.
Domestic producers would lose because production
would decline and the price in the market would also
fall.

(b) Domestic consumption would fall by an amount equal to
CE units.
Domestic production would increase by an amount
equal to AB units.
Price would increase to $500, an increase of $200.

Domestic producers would gain from additional units
supplied at a higher price.
Domestic consumers would lose because of higher prices
and fewer units available.

4. The type of argument being used is the cheap foreign labor
argument. This argument may be incorrect for three reasons:
(a) labor is only one of the factors of production; (b) low wages
imply low productivity; and (c) the argument ignores the
concept of comparative advantage.

Chapter 11

THE PROBLEMS OF TRADE

IMPORTANT TERMS AND CONCEPTS

appreciation
balance-of-payments problem
Classical Gold-Flow Model
common market
depreciation
devaluation
domestic gold standard
exchange rate
fixed exchange-rate system

flexible exchange rate system
international gold standard
International Monetary Fund
    (IMF)
modified gold-fixed exchange
    rate system
Quantity Theory of Money
velocity of money

COMPLETION QUESTIONS

Fill in the blanks with the proper word or words from the list above. Not all terms are used.

1. The _____ was established at the Bretton Woods Conference.

2. The _____ stated that money supply and prices rise and fall together.

3. With the _____ , the world's currencies are subject to supply-demand markets.

4. The "price" of a currency is its _____.

5. The _____ dominated the international scene for almost 30 years.

6. There would never be a _____ if all countries used the same currency.

7. For the _____ to have worked, all the countries involved in trade had to be on an international gold standard as well as on a domestic gold standard.

8. The _____ is the number of times an average dollar changes hands during a year.

9. At the 1944 Bretton Woods conference, it was agreed that the world would be on a(n) _____.

CROSSWORD PUZZLE

Fill in the crossword puzzle from the list of Important Terms and Concepts. Not all terms are used.

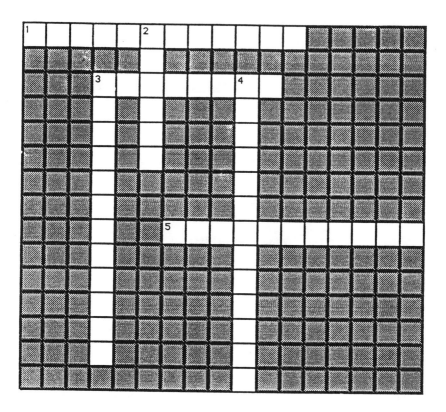

ACROSS
1. Increase in the value of a currency.
3. Gold standard within one country.
5. Depreciation against all currencies.

DOWN
2. ———— market, is a collection of European markets.
3. Decrease in the value of a currency.
4. Gold standard among countries.

TRUE AND FALSE

_____ 1. Even though U.S. productivity growth has slowed significantly, the American output per worker hour is still higher than in most other industrialized countries.

_____ 2. More than 85 percent of the United States' GNP is due to foreign trade.

_____ 3. The Bretton Woods fixed exchange rate philosophy was not compatible with current international trade realities after 1971.

_____ 4. The efforts to "tie" foreign aid to the purchase of U.S. goods cured the balance-of-payments problem.

_____ 5. Using a gold exchange system has its limitations because of the relatively fixed supply of gold.

_____ 6. The Common Market helped increase U.S. exports.

_____ 7. The Europeans and Japanese have widened the "productivity gap" that existed after World War II.

_____ 8. The fixed exchange rate system had a structural inability to effectively deal with the possible devaluation of the dollar.

_____ 9. The overwhelming major flaw of the modified gold-fixed exchange rate system was its reliance on the dollar.

_____10. A currency will be "devalued" when a country keeps running chronic balance-of-payments deficits.

MULTIPLE CHOICE

1. Dollars were a kind of world "legal tender" under the
   a. modified gold standard
   b. classical gold-flow period
   c. current period
   d. David Ricardo plan
   e. none of the above

2. It was agreed at the 1944 Bretton Woods Conference that the world was to be on a(n)
   a. fixed exchange rate system using the dollar as the centerpiece currency

97

b. fixed exchange rate system using gold as the center piece
c. flexible exchange
d. classical system
e. none of the above

3. Appreciation is

a. inflation
b. deflation
c. the opposite of depreciation
d. debasement
e. all of the above

4. As dollars depreciate relative to the mark,

a. Germany now sees U.S. exports as less expensive.
b. Americans should begin to cut back their German purchases.
c. The German mark appreciates.
d. all of the above
e. none of the above

5. Germany will supply us with marks according to

a. our treaty
b. their desire to purchase U.S. products
c. the common market standard
d. all of the above
e. none of the above

6. According to the Classical Gold-Flow Model, if a country's imports are greater than its exports,

a. that country's gold reserve will drop
b. that country's money supply will drop
c. prices in that country will fall
d. exports from that country will increase
e. all of the above

7. We are no longer on an international gold standard nor is our domestic money supply backed by gold because

a. there is not enough gold available
b. prices do not respond with the flexibility needed to make the system work

c. the Quantity Theory of Money may not work as believed
d. all of the above
e. none of the above

8. The Quantity Theory of Money assumed that
   a. $M = V$
   b. $P = Q$
   c. P and V move together
   d. M and P move together
   e. Q and V are not constant

9. Trade between countries ought to roughly "balance out" over time; otherwise, the surplus country will
   a. go broke
   b. build up unwanted foreign currencies
   c. build up a foreign currency deficit
   d. increase trade
   e. none of the above

10. The balance-of-payments problem would not exist if all countries
    a. used the same currencies
    b. did not trade
    c. used barter to trade
    d. all of the above
    e. none of the above

PROBLEMS AND DISCUSSION

1. Use the Quantity Theory of Money and the following data to answer questions (a) and (b):

Money Supply M	Velocity V	Price Level P	Volume Goods Q
$6	2	$3	4

a. If V and Q are constant, what will the price level be if M increases to $12?

b. If V and Q are constant, what will the price level be if M decreases to $2?

2. Illustrate on the following figure what would happen to the mark exchange rate if Americans decided to demand fewer German products or decided to travel less in Germany.

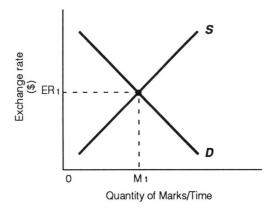

Quantity of Marks/Time

3. The following figure shows a hypothetical exchange rate market where U.S. dollars and Japanese yen are traded. The market is originally in equilibrium at $.003/yen with Q_1 yen being exchanged. Given this information, solve problems (a), (b), and (c):

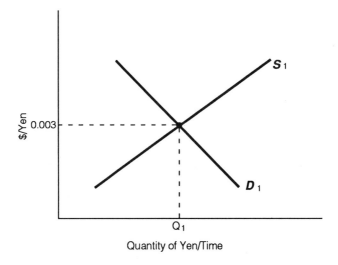

Quantity of Yen/Time

(a) On the figure, show the effects of a decrease in the supply of yen together with an increase in the demand for yen.

(b) Given the changes in problem 3(a), if the exchange rate were allowed to float freely, would the U.S. dollar appreciate or depreciate? Would the Japanese yen appreciate or depreciate?

(c) If the dollar/yen rate were pegged at $.003 by Japanese authorities, what action would be necessary in order that the exchange rate remain at the pegged level?

4. Assume that you have just received 50 video cassette recorders from Hanyo Incorporated in Japan. You expect to sell these VCRs at a special introductory price of $300 each this weekend. Hanyo has invoiced you for the 30 VCRs for a total amount of 3,375,000 yen. The invoice is to be paid in thirty days and must be paid in yen. You check the *Wall Street Journal* and find that the present (spot) exchange rate is 250 yen per dollar and the 30-day forward rate is 270 yen per dollar. What should you do in order to maximize your profit on this sale of VCRs?

Chapter 11
ANSWERS

COMPLETION QUESTIONS

1. International Monetary Fund
2. Quantity Theory of Money
3. flexible exchange rate system
4. exchange rate
5. modified gold-fixed exchange rate system
6. balance-of-payments problem
7. Classical Gold-Flow Model
8. velocity of money
9. fixed exchange-rate system

CROSSWORD PUZZLE

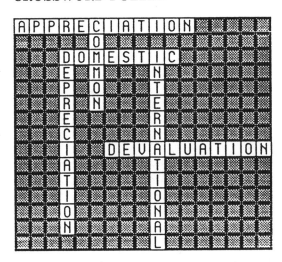

TRUE AND FALSE

1. true
2. false
3. true
4. false
5. true
6. false
7. false
8. true
9. true
10. true

MULTIPLE CHOICE

1. a	6. e
2. a	7. d
3. c	8. d
4. d	9. b
5. b	10. d

PROBLEMS AND DISCUSSION

1. a. $MV = PQ$

$$\$12 \times 2 = P \times 4$$
$$\$24 = 4P$$
$$P = \frac{\$24}{4} = \$6$$

   b. $MV = PQ$

$$\$2 \times 2 = P \times 4$$
$$\$4 = 4P$$
$$P = \frac{\$4}{4} = \$1$$

2.

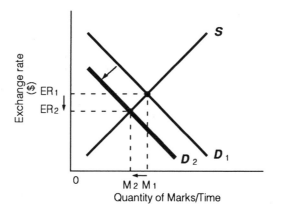

3. (a)

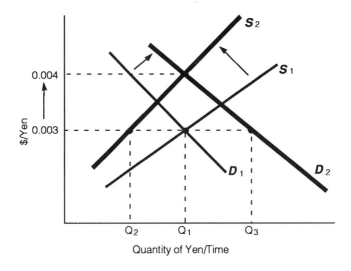

Quantity of Yen/Time

(b) The dollar/yen exchange rate would rise above the present level of $.003 to some other rate, such as $.004 (shown on the figure above). It would now require a larger amount of U.S. dollars to buy one Japanese yen. Therefore, the dollar depreciates (loses value) while the yen appreciates (gains value).

(c) Japanese authorities would be required to supply yen at $.003 because private demand exceeds private supply at the pegged rate. The amount of yen supplied by Japanese authorities would have to be $Q_3 - Q_2$. These yen would be supplied by the Japanese authorities to buy dollars in excess supply.

4. You have two options: First, you can buy 3,375,000 yen in the spot market at a rate of 250 yen per dollar. The necessary amount of yen would cost $13,500 dollars and you would simply hold the yen until it was time to pay for the invoice. Or you could pay the invoice early. Second, you could enter into a forward exchange contract agreeing to purchase 3,375,000 yen in 30 days at a price of 270 yen per dollar. In 30 days, you would get the necessary amount of yen for $12,500 and pay Hanyo at that time. There are two advantages to using the forward exchange market in this example.

First, the cost of the yen is $1,000 less, and, second, you have the $12,500 to use for the 30-day period and presumably could earn interest by investing it for a short time in some risk-free situation.

If you buy yen in the spot market, your gross profit would be $1,500.

Chapter 12

WORLD DEVELOPMENT

IMPORTANT TERMS AND CONCEPTS

Gaia Theory
institutional barriers
less developed countries
mass illiteracy
mass world poverty
multinational corporations
nutrition problem
population

productive capital
productivity
Third World countries
vicious circle of underdevelopment
wealth and income distribution

COMPLETION QUESTIONS

Fill in the blanks with the proper word or words from the list above. Not all terms are used.

1. The problem of _____ must be considered the major economic issue of our time.

2. The _____ traps many countries into a Third World status.

3. _____ to change include adverse power relationships, elitist political systems, and cultural traditions.

4. The _____ in poor countries result(s) in diseases such as kwashiorkor and zerophthalmia.

5. The regions of Asia (except Japan and Taiwan), Black Africa, and Latin America are known as _____ or _____.

6. The fact that most education resources in less developed countries go to the elite class results in _____.

7. Because of _____ , domestic manufacturing in Third World countries may be stifled.

CROSSWORD PUZZLE

Fill in the crossword puzzle from the list of Important Terms and Concepts. Not all terms are used.

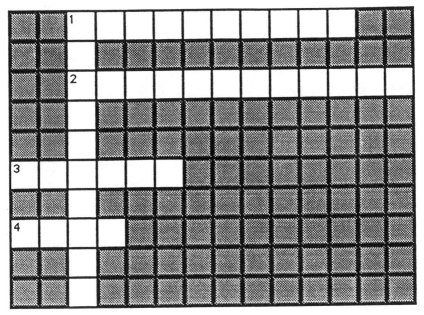

ACROSS
1. Capital embodies technical advances.
2. Output per unit of input.
3. _____ and income distribution differences are great.
4. _____ theory is the planet as self regulating system.

DOWN
1. _____ problems exist when birth rates are high.

TRUE AND FALSE

_____ 1. The major problem in development economics today is how the highly developed countries can help bring about the necessary changes in the poorest countries.

_____ 2. Poor countries should not waste their money by encouraging national savings.

_____ 3. With a lopsided distribution of wealth and the dominance of foreign interest, there is often little incentive for local economic development in poor countries.

_____ 4. Although foreign investments in less developed countries may bring about some temporary employment advantages, the long-run benefits to the poor are questionable.

_____ 5. Economic assistance for less developed countries should be the kind of aid that finances capital-intensive projects such as dam building.

_____ 6. The best and least repressive method in reversing people's attitudes about family size is to bring about economic development.

_____ 7. In less developed countries a large family provides for future "social security."

_____ 8. There are no differences between the poor of Third World countries and those of industrialized countries.

_____ 9. Poor education and nutritional deficiencies ultimately reduce the potential productivity of human resources.

_____10. The needs of the Third World farmer are really no different from those of farmers elsewhere; i.e., good economic incentives.

MULTIPLE CHOICE

1. Many students from less developed countries
   a. choose "literate" professions or civil training
   b. receive legal or medical training
   c. eventually serve an upper-class clientele
   d. all of the above
   e. none of the above

2. The economic incentives to farmers in many less developed countries are

    a. blocked due to elitist land-tenure arrangements and artificially low prices

    b. helped by a self-reliant agrarian base

    c. reinforced by the capital-intensive nature of their economic systems

    d. all of the above

    e. none of the above

3. The "vicious circle of underdevelopment" includes

    a. low productivity

    b. low incomes

    c. low levels of consumption

    d. both a and b are false

    e. a, b, and c are true

4. The best estimates indicate that there will be _____ billion people by the year 2000.

    a. 1

    b. 6

    c. 4 1/2

    d. 8

    e. 12

5. Poor countries are usually agrarian societies in which more than _____ percent of the population work and live in rural areas.

    a. 100

    b. 90

    c. 75

    d. 95

    e. 85

PROBLEMS AND DISCUSSION

1. Why are foreigners who "stayed behind" in former colonies a problem for the development of Third World countries?

2. What can be done about the "institutional barriers" to development?

3. Have the issues concerning "global warming" been solved by scientists and governments?

Chapter 12
ANSWERS

COMPLETION QUESTIONS

1. mass world poverty
2. vicious circle of underdevelopment
3. institutional barriers
4. nutrition problem
5. Third World countries,
less developed countries
6. mass illiteracy
7. multinational corpora-
tions

CROSSWORD PUZZLE

```
    P R O D U C T I V E
    O
    P R O D U C T I V I T Y
    U
    L
W E A L T H
    T
G A I A
    O
    N
```

TRUE AND FALSE

1. true	6. true
2. false	7. true
3. true	8. false
4. true	9. true
5. false	10. true

MULTIPLE CHOICE

1. d
2. a
3. e
4. b
5. c

PROBLEMS AND DISCUSSION

1. Many foreigners who "stayed behind" in the former colonies now own immense parcels of property. They also often control the corporations that exploit the raw materials of the country. This leads to dependency, unequal growth, and a reliance on one or two exports to earn foreign exchange.

2. The land-tenure relationships, effective programs of population control, health and hygienic improvements, an improved education system, the emergence of local entrepreneurs, and the encouragement of national savings are all necessary to begin the process of development.

3. No, many different scientists have come to different conclusions concerning global warming. Governments have in general been very slow to enact policies and laws, in part due to the inconclusive nature of the scientific evidence. Some people believe that we should not wait for "scientific proof" before we take steps to correct the problem.